5-Minute Manifesting Journal

5-Minute Manifesting Journal

Focus Your Mind, Raise Your Vibration, and Turn Your Dreams into Reality

Scott Moore

 ROCKRIDGE PRESS

TO MY MOM, THE PHOENIX.

For general information on our other products and services or to obtain technical support, please contact our Customer Care Department within the United States at (866) 744-2665, or outside the United States at (510) 253-0500.

Rockridge Press publishes its books in a variety of electronic and print formats. Some content that appears in print may not be available in electronic books, and vice versa.

TRADEMARKS: Rockridge Press and the Rockridge Press logo are trademarks or registered trademarks of Callisto Media Inc. and/or its affiliates, in the United States and other countries, and may not be used without written permission. All other trademarks are the property of their respective owners. Rockridge Press is not associated with any product or vendor mentioned in this book.

Cover Designer: Carlos Esparza
Interior Designer: Jennifer Hsu
Art Producer: Tom Hood
Editor: Adrian Potts
Production Editor: Andrew Yackira
Production Manager: Jose Olivera

Author photograph courtesy of Alex Adams

ISBN: Print 978-1-63807-095-5
R0

Contents

Introduction

I was freaking out. My lease was up, and unless I found a new apartment soon, I'd have nowhere to live. It wasn't like I hadn't searched for apartments. I had. In fact, I'd seen dozens of them—but they all had huge problems that made living in them an impossibility for me.

Then it dawned on me: I wasn't even sure what I was looking for. And if I didn't know what I was looking for, how would I possibly know when I found the right apartment? I immediately pulled out a pen and paper, and wrote down *exactly* what I wanted in an apartment. I listed 15 *very* specific criteria, including the monthly rent, neighborhood where the apartment was located, and that it would have parking and laundry facilities. I even included ridiculously specific details like architectural style, construction era, and that I wanted it to have arched doorways.

The very next day, I went to look at one more apartment. This apartment met *every single one* of my criteria, down to the construction dates. I couldn't believe it!

This is just one example of manifesting, which is the process of transforming your hopes and wishes into reality through the power of the mind. But don't be fooled—manifesting isn't always as easy as just making a list. Rather, the simple work of writing down my desires opened me up to greater possibilities.

What made this experience different from simply passively hoping I'd find a good apartment? I used specificity in calling out exactly what I needed to the universe, I trusted in the universe that what I wanted was attainable, and I engaged in the action of writing it down. These simple but crucial steps helped tell the universe that I was not messing around, and that I was an active participant in creating what I desired. These steps can be applied to any realm of your life, be it family, home, work, creative endeavors, or anything else (we'll get into the details in a few pages).

Much of my thinking on manifesting has been informed by my 20-some years of work as a licensed yoga and meditation teacher. Through my practice and teaching, I have observed our innate human capacity to connect the body, mind, and spirit to become who we are destined to be.

Using this journal for five minutes each day will serve you in many ways. Whether you are a manifesting expert, a novice, would like to get back into practice, or are simply intrigued by the possibilities, this journal can be a catalyst for expansive personal growth. It can help you if you are going through a hard time, feeling stuck, or just looking to take the time to include more intentional, thoughtful, and focused practices in your day. It will help you clarify what you want in life, and put a message out to the universe that you're ready and willing to see these kinds of changes in your life.

Although this journal can be a great way to work through complicated feelings, if you are experiencing ongoing or debilitating feelings of anxiety or depression, these conditions should be addressed by medical professionals. This book is not intended to be a replacement for your therapist, medication, or medical treatment. It's honorable to seek help and treatment when or if you need it.

You're about to begin a wonderful journey that will transport you miles down the road to who you are destined to become. The simple action of writing words on a page creates magic that can transform your life in ways that are both small and large.

Your life is a cosmic chess game, and it's your turn to move!

PART I

Manifesting 101

Manifesting is immensely empowering because it provides a simple and tangible way for you to co-create the kind of life you wish to see for yourself. It also serves as an enlightening filter through which you may discover the relationship between yourself and the universe, or view it in a new way. By learning to manifest every day, you will start to see how you and the universe conspire together for your own success.

What Is Manifesting?

Manifesting is the spiritual idea that you can turn your goals, desires, and dreams into reality through visualization, meditation, and other techniques that help you harness the power of the mind. It's about writing the future you'd like to see for yourself. Manifesting is less about wishful or fanciful thinking, and more about leveraging the law of attraction to *co-create* the life that you know you are destined to live.

Manifesting may sometimes assist you in solving a very specific and practical problem, like finding the perfect apartment. It might also help you find your life partner, or discover and excel in the vocation that will enable you to share your gifts with the world. Although manifesting can be associated with material goods and wealth, it's less about what you may acquire, and more about evolving into the you that is destined to have the kind of life you know is waiting for you.

How Does Manifesting Work?

Manifesting can impact every area of our lives: relationships, opportunities, self-love, self-worth, achieving goals, career and personal success, love, etc. As you consider the kind of life you'd like to manifest for yourself, it's essential to take small steps forward every day and to be patient, understanding that the universe may be on a different timeline than you.

The process of manifesting can be broken down into a few key steps: clarifying your vision, knowing what to ask of the universe and how to speak with it, and learning to ride waves of opportunity.

CLARIFYING YOUR VISION

Manifesting is about getting crystal clear with what you want, then being bold enough to suggest it to the universe by simply writing it down on paper. If you haven't discovered this already, you'll likely be astounded by how powerfully this simple practice can manifest what you'd like to see in your life.

One problem that most of us face is that we are too vague about what we want from life. Many of us want to have a "good life" without really defining exactly what "good" means to us.

I believe that many of us are afraid to actually quantify what we want, because we are afraid that the disappointment of knowing what we want but not getting it will be painful. But to enact the power of manifesting, we need to start by drilling down on exactly what it is we want. Understanding and envisioning exactly what you want helps you refine what you're looking for, and lets you know when you've found it.

Clarifying your vision might start through the use of some simple tools, such as creatively brainstorming lists of possibilities with trusted friends or family members, creating vision boards filled with images that remind you of what you'd like to manifest, and by meditating upon and visualizing what you'd like to see for yourself.

Many of the things you may wish to manifest in your life may already be very close at hand (as my perfect apartment was). For larger or seemingly out-of-reach goals, it's important to remember that the materials to build the life you want *are* within reach. Start simple, start today, and grow into tomorrow.

KNOWING WHAT TO ASK

Manifesting is less about magically conjuring something for yourself, and more about stepping into your own power, telling the universe exactly what you'd like and perhaps even suggesting ways to get it. It's helpful to be as specific as possible. Simply clarifying what you want and asking for it demonstrates some thought and action on your part.

Maybe you'd like to get that raise or promotion you've been hoping for, or optimize your relationships with your partner, spouse, family members, or friends. What are the life goals that you'd like to accomplish before you die? Whatever it is, ask for it!

It's also important to remember that the process of manifesting isn't simply about putting in your order to the universe and waiting around for it to fall into your lap. You have a big responsibility in bringing about what you would like to manifest, too.

SPEAKING WITH THE UNIVERSE

A powerful way of asking the universe for what you'd like is by making a positive statement of truth, such as "I am on my way to _____." Through writing your intentions in this journal, you'll learn the power of making these positive statements of truth. The universe exists as one big "yes." A positive statement of truth leverages this universal "yes" to put a little "yes-sauce" on what you'd like to see in your life. Since the universe is a "yes," it doesn't understand "no" and therefore doesn't respond as well to avoiding things you don't want. So direct your energy toward what you'd like to manifest, rather than what you'd like to avoid. For example, when you ask to avoid getting yet another messy roommate, you're still focused on messy roommates. Instead, ask for a clean roommate.

RIDING THE WAVE OF "YES"

Manifesting is surfing the wave of the universal "yes." I like this analogy because it suggests that, just like riding a wave, you're in *conversation* with the universe, rather than trying to control it. Just as surfers can learn to work with the power of the ocean's waves, when you learn to not only avoid being pummeled by the waves of life but also actually ride them, you exist in a beautiful, symbiotic relationship with something immense and powerful.

Manifesting in Action: Tim's Story

I often lead yoga and meditation retreats around the world, including many retreats at my uncle's ranch, a cozy cabin nestled in the deeply forested Uinta mountains. During the cabin retreats, we hold a ceremony in which each person is invited to envision and speak about what they wish to see for themselves in the next five years. At one retreat, Tim, a relatively young lawyer, expressed his desire to advance in his career and one day become a judge. After the ceremony, I encouraged everyone to journal about their desires and regularly revisit them as a way of watching their own progress. Five years after this retreat, Tim did in fact become a judge, and he pulled me aside to tell me that he felt that his experience of calling out his intentions in that sacred ceremony, then writing them down in his journal, allowed him to clarify his vision and begin the journey to manifest his dream.

The Key Concepts

At first glance, manifesting can seem vague. But there are some concrete principles at play that can help your manifestation practice become more actionable and transformational. These concepts include gratitude, the law of attraction, raising your vibration, and understanding your journey.

THE IMPORTANCE OF GRATITUDE

Gratitude is a key part of the manifestation process. It is the opposite of expectation—gratitude acknowledges what you've been given, whereas expectation creates a feeling of being owed something. Focusing on gratitude for what you have and what you are anchors you solidly in the "yes" of the universe, which can drive more "yes" your way.

One of the reasons that gratitude is such an essential concept in manifesting is because of how it changes your own heart. Gratitude is an antidote to selfishness, bitterness, and expectations—all of which can trap us in a vortex of negativity.

THE LAW OF ATTRACTION

Ever notice how happy people seem to attract other happy people, and miserable people seem to attract other miserable people? This happens due to the universal Law of Attraction. The Law of Attraction, which states that like energy attracts like energy, plays a big role in manifesting. Therefore, showing up in the world in the way that you'd like the universe to show up for you needs to be a daily practice. This truth cannot be overstated.

One of the ways I practice attracting more generosity toward my own life is by leaving generous tips. I often leave a $5 tip for a latte that costs me only $4. It's incredible how often this generates more generosity coming into my own life.

The Law of Attraction gives you a way to change your outlook and approach in all situations. If you're looking for more abundance in your life, you may need to become aware of, then reevaluate, your beliefs around scarcity. If you're looking for more lasting, respectful, or loving relationships in your life, you might need to work on finding new ways to share your love with the world. Begin to exhibit the qualities you'd like to see manifest in your life in whatever ways you can, and see how like attracts like.

RAISING YOUR VIBRATION

A vibration is simply a frequency of movement. Everything in existence, from the smallest particle to the largest galaxy, has a vibration. Colors, sounds, emotions, and even actions have vibrations. *You* have a vibration. Learning to recognize and tune your vibration to receive the things you'd like in your life is a key component of manifesting.

This concept can be understood by exploring the principle of sympathetic vibration. This means one thing resonating in tandem with another thing that is similarly tuned, like a guitar string that vibrates when another instrument is playing the same note. Similarly, when you meet people that resonate with you, or take in a speech, movie, or play that inspires you, you are moved because you are tuned in a similar way.

You can tune yourself to resonate with the kinds of qualities you would like to see manifest in your life. This can be done simply, by doing things like committing to this five-minute daily journaling practice; eating healthy, life-rich foods; using uplifting speech; getting enough sleep; exercising regularly; and practicing yoga and meditation. Remember that what you're manifesting is the version of yourself that holds the highest vibration, not just the version of yourself that has the highest income.

The Benefits of a Consistent Practice

As I consider the things that I've manifested in my life, I recognize that many of the fruits I'm enjoying now are the result of the seeds I planted many years ago—sometimes decades ago. Not everything we wish to manifest in our lives will happen immediately. Consider each entry in your journal to be a seed. Some of them will sprout right away, whereas others might not begin to grow for many years. Either way, you're on your way.

THE GIFT OF FIVE MINUTES

Some may wonder how a practice of only five minutes could possibly be enough. In fact, there is enormous power in a small practice, especially when it is coupled with the catalytic power of consistency.

When accomplishing a big task, breaking it down into smaller, simpler tasks is often the best way to begin to tackle it. Five minutes of daily journaling gives you something simple and concrete to do in the immediate moment. It gets you moving on your journey.

As you continue to do your five minutes daily, you will soon look back and realize that you've actually accomplished something quite large.

Tools to Enhance Your Experience

As a yoga and meditation teacher, I understand the value of creating sacred space. Your state of mind and the setting in which you practice your journaling ritual will have a large effect on its impact for you. Even though your journaling may take only five minutes, treat it as the sacred practice that it is. As such, you may wish to create a sacred space to enhance your experience.

I encourage you to choose a special space and/or time for your journaling practice, and to do your best to maintain this ritual. You may choose to light candles, burn incense, or place crystals, statues, or photographs of your teachers or spiritual leaders near your writing space. None of these elements are necessary for the practice, but if you feel called to use them, they may make the experience more impactful.

The Role of Reflection and Writing

Writing and reflecting is a transformative practice. The practice of writing in your journal helps you focus your mind, connect with your true self, and easily track your progress.

FOCUSING YOUR MIND

With email, social media, cell phones, and TV all vying for our attention, it's no wonder that so many of us find it hard to focus these days. Journaling is a great way to remove yourself from distractions and pay attention to a single task. When you cut out the noise of daily living and focus on the contents of a journal, you are better able to absorb important messages in your mind and psyche. Finding space to reflect on and write about your thoughts and feelings encourages you to be more deliberate about what it is you want out of life and how to achieve it. In the world of manifesting, taking a thought, forming it into words, and putting it on a page is how an idea begins to become real.

CONNECT TO YOUR TRUE SELF

The ancient Indian tradition of Vedic wisdom says that our true identity is consciousness itself. Therefore, all practices—including yoga, meditation, and manifesting through a journal—are the mechanisms and crafts that deepen your consciousness and connect you with your true self.

Vedic wisdom also posits that consciousness precedes form—so if you can think it, and even go so far as to write it down, you are well on your way to helping it take shape in your life. As you tap into the greater consciousness of your true self, you'll find yourself writing things you didn't know you knew.

TRACK YOUR PROGRESS

One of the greatest features of this manifesting journal is the simple ability to track your progress. As you work through the journal, you'll notice that the prompts and practices invite you to reach a little further in your manifesting. As time goes on, you will find the practice flowing more easily. You'll also be thrilled to find interesting synchronicities and events that respond to the things you are writing. And of course, when you're done with the journal, you'll look back and be proud of the person you've become through the process.

How to Use This Journal

Each day, this journal contains space for you to write about what you are grateful for, what you are manifesting, and what you are reflecting on. To inspire you each day, there is a brief prompt or practice around an aspect of manifesting, along with an affirmation for you to repeat to yourself while completing each page.

It helps to be as plain and direct as possible in your words when you write. Don't get too hung up on punctuation, spelling, or editing. Just keep writing. The process of making your words flow is what lets the magic begin to happen. To this end, it may help for you to set a timer and write without stopping. As you remain in the flow of writing, you give yourself over to the muse, that powerful goddess who will help you manifest. It's also useful to choose a certain time to do your journaling. I suggest writing at the same time every day.

If you ever find yourself staring at the page blankly, pen in hand, frozen without the slightest notion of what to write, I suggest using a technique that I learned from my generative writing coach, Nan: Simply keep the pen moving. If ever you get stuck, just start writing whatever comes to mind. Or begin with the phrase "I'm creating for myself . . ." or "What I really want to say is . . ." Both of these phrases are great ways to keep the pen in motion, and you'll soon find yourself back in the flow of writing.

You're Ready to Start

You're now ready to begin your manifestation journey. Remember that despite the simple sacredness of this practice, it *is* fundamentally a practice, not something to perfect. Allow this journal to be a work in progress. Avoid the perfectionist mindset and let this practice flow and evolve however it needs to flow and evolve. Just stay committed and connected to the process, and keep your mind open and alert to the subtle and sometimes overt ways that you are creating wonderful change in your life.

I acknowledge you for being on this path of self-discovery and manifestation. And I am eager for you to create the kind of life you have always wanted, and become the person that you are destined to become.

DATE: *November 17, 2021*

I am grateful for: *Today, I'm grateful for the incredible potential that is within me.*

How might you be preventing yourself from becoming the person you know you are destined to become? Today is the day to acknowledge your light and shine.

I am manifesting: *Stepping into my confidence so that I am happy, focused, and open to opportunities.*

I am reflecting on: *I'm committed to starting a five-minute meditation each day this week to help center my thoughts and focus. If/when I encounter speed bumps, I know that I have the inner resources to succeed.*

Sample Journal Entry

I AM LIGHT AND THE WORLD NEEDS ME TO SHINE.

Your Daily Journal Entries

Part II of this book is the journal that you will be writing in every day. You'll see space to enter the date, an opportunity to list what you are grateful for that day, and a brief prompt or practice that is designed to inspire. There is space to respond to the prompt, as well as a brief section to note what specifically you are manifesting. You can also note other reflections you might have. The page will end with an affirmation that you can take with you for the rest of the day. I encourage you to commit to this practice every day, for five minutes a day. I am confident that with this simple and regular practice, you will see big and lasting changes occur in your life.

Thank you for being on this journey with me. Let's begin!

DATE: *Tuesday November 15th 2022*

I am grateful for: Maddy & her family. I am grateful for the moments my loved ones understood me.

Your vibration is the product of many factors, including the words you use, music you listen to, food you eat, media you absorb, and people you associate with. Today, tune your frequency to reflect your highest being.

I am manifesting: A happy strong soul fulfilled and experienced with all my heart's hopes and dreams.

I am reflecting on: Pain, defeating thoughts & my difficulty letting go of things that hurt. Trust issues.

I RESONATE AT A HIGH VIBRATION.

DATE:

I am grateful for:

The universe is conspiring for your success. Many things that you are not aware of are quietly working behind the scenes to help you thrive.

I am manifesting:

I am reflecting on:

DATE:

I am grateful for:

There's never been anyone else like you on this earth. You are as miraculous and special as any king or queen who has ever lived.

I am manifesting:

I am reflecting on:

MY UNIQUENESS IS ONE OF MY GREATEST STRENGTHS.

DATE:

I am grateful for:

Self-care is perhaps the most altruistic action a person can take. This is because it ensures the survival—and even prosperity—of a vital world resource: YOU.

I am manifesting:

I am reflecting on:

CARING FOR MYSELF IS ONE OF THE WAYS THAT I CARE FOR THE WORLD.

17

I am grateful for: _____

_____

There is only ever this moment. "Now" represents reality, since the past and future are abstractions. The only way to live in reality is to be here.

I am manifesting: _____

_____

_____

I am reflecting on: _____

_____

_____

I AM AWARE THAT I AM AWARE.

DATE:

I am grateful for:

Nobody invented dancing; they simply learned to ride the wave of its power. How can you allow yourself to dance with life today?

I am manifesting:

I am reflecting on:

I AM RIDING THE WAVE OF CREATIVITY.

19

DATE:

I am grateful for:

Consider a problem you are working with. Be as creative as possible as you think of solutions.

I am manifesting:

I am reflecting on:

CREATIVITY IS THE ANSWER TO ANY PROBLEM.

I am grateful for:

Consider all the quiet acts of kindness that are silently happening all around your community. What do you notice and how can you participate?

I am manifesting:

I am reflecting on:

KINDNESS IS A SUPERPOWER.

DATE:

I am grateful for:

Reach for the stars with your feet firmly planted on the ground. Practice manifesting your dream using the practical tools at your fingertips.

I am manifesting:

I am reflecting on:

THE WORK I DO IS BUILDING
A BEAUTIFUL LIFE FOR MYSELF.

DATE:

I am grateful for:

When do you feel your best? Think about one moment where you felt on top of the world. How can you re-create that feeling today?

I am manifesting:

I am reflecting on:

I AM ON THE ROAD TO BECOMING THE BEST POSSIBLE VERSION OF MYSELF.

DATE:

I am grateful for:

To love another person, you must love yourself. If you were your own friend, what kind of a friend would you be?

I am manifesting:

I am reflecting on:

**NO MATTER WHAT HAPPENS IN MY LIFE,
I CAN ALWAYS TURN TO LOVE.**

DATE:

I am grateful for:

Your work is one of the best ways to discover your personal gifts. Using your unique gifts, how do you see yourself growing in your career?

I am manifesting:

I am reflecting on:

MY PRIMARY WORK IN THIS LIFE IS TO GROW.

I am grateful for:

There is no limit to what is possible when a person is rooted in love. Your heart contains an inexhaustible amount of energy.

I am manifesting:

I am reflecting on:

LOVE IS THE GREATEST FORCE IN THE UNIVERSE.

I am grateful for:

It is not a question of whether or not you will become the great person you are des-tined to become; it's only a question of when. What are you waiting for?

I am manifesting:

I am reflecting on:

**EVERY DAY, I'M EVOLVING INTO THE PERSON
THAT I AM DESTINED TO BECOME.**

I am grateful for:

Raising your vibration is as simple as changing your mindset from "I can't" to "I can." The universe vibrates at a frequency of "YES!"

I am manifesting:

I am reflecting on:

MY POSITIVITY IS MY SUPERPOWER.

I am grateful for:

Do you welcome change, or find it difficult to deal with? Either way, be grateful for the opportunity to wake up and make that decision each day.

I am manifesting:

I am reflecting on:

EACH STEP FORWARD IS A MIRACLE.

DATE:

I am grateful for: _____

_____

The universe was set into motion and has evolved for you to fall in love with this very moment.

I am manifesting: _____

_____

_____

I am reflecting on: _____

_____

_____

I AM EXACTLY WHERE I NEED TO BE IN THIS MOMENT.

I am grateful for:

All day, we train other people to love us based on the way that we love ourselves.

I am manifesting:

I am reflecting on:

I HAVE LIMITLESS LOVE WITHIN ME.

DATE:

I am grateful for:

What are the conditions that you need to thrive? Prioritize self-care every day, in both large and small ways.

I am manifesting:

I am reflecting on:

EACH DAY IS ANOTHER OPPORTUNITY TO GROW.

I am grateful for:

Spend a few minutes each day creating a mood/vision board. Search for images online or in magazines that depict some of the things you'd like to manifest in your life. Display this board in a prominent place, so that you see it regularly. Seeing is believing, and believing is the key to manifesting.

I am manifesting:

I am reflecting on:

MY LIFE IS BEAUTIFUL, SATISFYING, JOYOUS.

DATE:

I am grateful for:

Visualize your greatest goal for the next year, the next 5 years, the next 10 years, and beyond. Give yourself a moment or two of reflection on each goal, then write them down on a piece of paper. Revisit this list regularly, even on a weekly basis.

I am manifesting:

I am reflecting on:

MY LIFE IS FULL OF POSSIBILITIES.

DATE:

I am grateful for:

Consider the career path, advancement, and growth you'd like to experience in your life. Close your eyes for a few moments and meditate on exactly *why* you desire that career path. Next, brainstorm any teachers, mentors, or role models you could choose to help you get to where you want to go. Finally, visualize how you will feel when you achieve that goal.

I am manifesting:

I am reflecting on:

**MY WORK IS ONE OF THE WAYS THAT
I SHOW LOVE TO THE WORLD.**

DATE:

I am grateful for:

Look for those opportunities that resonate with you as a "Hell, yeah!" rather than a "Maybe."

I am manifesting:

I am reflecting on:

**I MAINTAIN MY HIGH VIBRATION BY
NOT SETTLING FOR MEDIOCRITY.**

DATE:

I am grateful for:

You are right where you are meant to be. No matter your emotions, sit still, breathe, and give thanks for what you have in this moment—and all that will come in the next moment.

I am manifesting:

I am reflecting on:

**I AM GRATEFUL FOR WHAT HAS BEEN,
WHAT IS NOW, AND WHAT WILL BE.**

DATE: _____

_____

I am grateful for: _____

_____

Write yourself a love letter. Acknowledge the journey that has brought you to this moment and honor everything that you are.

I am manifesting: _____

_____

_____

I am reflecting on: _____

_____

_____

I AM EXACTLY WHO I AM SUPPOSED TO BE IN THIS MOMENT.

DATE:

I am grateful for:

Nobody understands your needs better than you do. Before you can take care of another person, you must first take care of yourself.

I am manifesting:

I am reflecting on:

**SELF-CARE IS NOT SELFISH; IT'S WHAT
I MUST DO TO HONOR MY INNATE VALUE.**

I am grateful for:

In this moment, there is as much opportunity to wake up to your ultimate destiny as there will ever be.

I am manifesting:

I am reflecting on:

**I AM WAKING UP TO THE PERSON THAT
I AM DESTINED TO BECOME.**

I am grateful for:

The universe has evolved over billions and billions of years to produce the inimitable you, and is using your hands to continue to build this world.

I am manifesting:

I am reflecting on:

I AM IMPORTANT BECAUSE I EXIST.

DATE:

I am grateful for:

What are all the ways you can be creative today? This could include what you choose to wear, the way you drive to work, or even a haiku you make up about the flowers you see along the way.

I am manifesting:

I am reflecting on:

MY LIFE IS A CREATIVE EXPRESSION.

DATE:

I am grateful for:

Today, change your mind state through meditation, breath, or gentle movement, and approach your problems from a new direction.

I am manifesting:

I am reflecting on:

**MY CREATIVITY IS MY BEST TOOL
FOR SOLVING ANY PROBLEM.**

DATE:

I am grateful for:

Close your eyes and take several deep breaths. Visualize the life of your breath flowing into whatever goal or achievement you wish to accomplish. Watch to see how this gives your efforts new life.

I am manifesting:

I am reflecting on:

I CAN INFUSE ANY AREA OF MY LIFE WITH ENERGY.

DATE:

I am grateful for:

Each member of a community is an essential element of a larger organism. That organism grows when each member is thriving.

I am manifesting:

I am reflecting on:

AS I GROW, MY COMMUNITY AROUND ME GROWS, TOO.

DATE:

I am grateful for:

There is as much potential for your genius to appear in this moment as in any other moment in history. Don't wait for a better moment to begin your masterpiece. Often, it's in the process that your genius arrives. Just start!

I am manifesting:

I am reflecting on:

TODAY, I CAN TAKE BOLD ACTIONS TOWARD MY DREAMS.

DATE:

I am grateful for:

Since body, mind, and spirit are all connected, and one part affects all others, you cannot change one without changing all. What are you doing today for your optimal wellness?

I am manifesting:

I am reflecting on:

**I AM ON THE ROAD TO OPTIMAL WELLNESS
IN BODY, MIND, AND SPIRIT.**

DATE:

I am grateful for:

Balanced energy is a better signifier of wellness than physical fitness. Notice the quality and quantity of energy you feel today. Does it feel balanced, or unfocused and jittery?

I am manifesting:

I am reflecting on:

MY ENERGY RADIATES WELLNESS.

DATE:

I am grateful for:

Every day, you are training others in how to treat you by showing them how you treat yourself—and by how you treat them.

I am manifesting:

I am reflecting on:

I ATTRACT THE LOVE I DESERVE BY LOVING MYSELF UNCONDITIONALLY.

DATE:

I am grateful for:

Consciousness precedes form. Imagining something is the first step to making it a reality.

I am manifesting:

I am reflecting on:

**I AM ATTRACTING POSITIVITY IN
MY LIFE BY THINKING POSITIVELY.**

DATE:

I am grateful for:

In a universe that is meant to thrive, one person's success does not require another person's failure.

I am manifesting:

I am reflecting on:

THE UNIVERSE ITSELF IS THE GREATEST
PROOF OF ABUNDANCE.

DATE:

I am grateful for:

Draw a line down the middle of a piece of paper. On the left, list your biggest failures. On the right, list what you have learned from each. Do not feel ashamed: Your failures are merely teaching tools, moving you toward your ultimate success.

I am manifesting:

I am reflecting on:

EACH FAILURE IS THE BIRTH OF A LARGER "YES."

DATE:

I am grateful for:

A sure way of raising the vibration of those around you is to be the kind of person that others want to resonate with. Rise up and bring others along with you.

I am manifesting:

I am reflecting on:

I'M ON MY WAY TO THE TOP, AND ANYONE I MEET IS COMING WITH ME.

I am grateful for:

Can you be grateful for things that have yet to happen? When you know that you are on a trajectory toward greatness, gratitude can lead you to your beautiful future.

I am manifesting:

I am reflecting on:

I AM BLESSED WITH OPPORTUNITIES AND POSSIBILITIES.

DATE:

I am grateful for:

The world exists as a love note from the universe, which is constantly whispering into your ear, "Look, my child! I made this for you."

I am manifesting:

I am reflecting on:

**TODAY, I CHOOSE TO SEE THE BEAUTY THAT
THE UNIVERSE IS SHOWING ME.**

DATE:

I am grateful for:

By regularly taking care of yourself, you're sending a message to the universe that you are doing your part to help yourself thrive.

I am manifesting:

I am reflecting on:

SELF-CARE IS ONE WAY THAT I LOVE MYSELF.

I am grateful for:

The only way to get "there," wherever "there" is, is to first be "here." To get to any destination, you have to travel by walking on the ground at your feet.

I am manifesting:

I am reflecting on:

HERE I AM.

I am grateful for:

Howard Thurman said, "Don't ask what the world needs. Ask what makes you come alive, and go do it. Because what the world needs is people who have come alive." What makes you come alive? That is your purpose.

I am manifesting:

I am reflecting on:

THE UNIVERSE IS SHOWING ME THE AVENUES THAT WILL ALLOW ME TO THRIVE.

I am grateful for:

The universe was creative enough to fill this planet with narwhals, nautiluses, and nightingales. What is the universe asking you to create?

I am manifesting:

I am reflecting on:

CREATIVITY IS MY SUPERPOWER.

DATE:

I am grateful for:

No problem is ever so big that it can't be broken into smaller steps. Going bit by bit, you'll start to make real progress.

I am manifesting:

I am reflecting on:

TODAY, I CAN TAKE A SMALL STEP FORWARD.

DATE:

I am grateful for:

You must use your creativity to comprehend what you are capable of achieving, then tap into your practicality to lay the plans that will help you make it into a reality.

I am manifesting:

I am reflecting on:

MY DREAMS ARE MY BLUEPRINTS, AND MY HANDS ARE THE WORKERS WHO'LL BUILD MY DREAM LIFE.

DATE: _____

I am grateful for: _____

_____

The masterpiece that is you is a collaborative project. You do not become your greatest self alone. How do you allow yourself to be molded by those around you?

I am manifesting: _____

_____

_____

I am reflecting on: _____

_____

_____

**MY COMMUNITY IS HELPING ME TO
GROW INTO MY GREATEST SELF.**

I am grateful for:

Sit, close your eyes, and think of a person who is important in your life. Then, repeat in your mind, "May you be safe. May you be well. May you be happy." Repeat this exercise three times: once on behalf of a loved one, once on behalf of a stranger, and once on behalf of someone with whom you have a difficult relationship.

I am manifesting:

I am reflecting on:

**THE HEARTBEAT OF THE WORLD IS
A RHYTHM OF COMPASSION.**

DATE:

I am grateful for:

The muse is constantly whispering ideas in your ear. Each idea holds a finite momentum and energy. If you do not act quickly, the energy dies and the muse whispers that idea to someone else.

I am manifesting:

I am reflecting on:

MY INSPIRATION LEADS ME TO ACTION.

DATE:

I am grateful for:

Wellness is more about balance than fitness. What are the ways you can create more balance in your life?

I am manifesting:

I am reflecting on:

I HAVE EVERYTHING I NEED FOR OPTIMAL WELLNESS INSIDE OF ME.

DATE:

I am grateful for: _____

_____

Whether consciously or unconsciously, you transmit energy to everyone around you. What kind of energy are you transmitting today?

I am manifesting: _____

_____

_____

I am reflecting on: _____

_____

_____

I'M SENDING POSITIVE ENERGY INTO THE WORLD.

DATE:

I am grateful for:

Ancient wisdom advises that our thoughts become our words, actions, habits, and character. Each of these things scripts our destiny. How are you writing your destiny?

I am manifesting:

I am reflecting on:

I AM CREATING THE UNIVERSE I CHOOSE TO LIVE IN.

DATE:

I am grateful for:

Pay little heed to either criticism or flattery. Find how freeing it can be to create for the pure joy of creativity.

I am manifesting:

I am reflecting on:

I DO NOT NEED PERMISSION FROM ANYONE TO THRIVE.

DATE:

I am grateful for:

Before making a decision, pause for a moment and notice how it makes you feel. Learn to feel as much as you think.

I am manifesting:

I am reflecting on:

I HAVE THE POWER OF TRUTH INSIDE OF ME.

DATE:

I am grateful for: _____

_____

On a piece of paper, make a list of three things you are grateful for (you can include what you wrote above, if you wish). Choose one and write a paragraph about why you're grateful for it.

I am manifesting: _____

_____

_____

I am reflecting on: _____

_____

_____

I AM BLESSED TO SEE THE ABUNDANCE ALL AROUND ME.

I am grateful for:

Before you can love another person, you must first learn to love yourself. If you do love others, it's because you have love within to offer another person.

I am manifesting:

I am reflecting on:

MY TRUEST ESSENCE IS THAT OF LOVE.

DATE:

I am grateful for:

Sometimes, self-care means doing something outrageous for yourself. What is a fantasy you have about something you'd like to do or have? Take a small step to honor it. Perhaps you might test-drive the car you'd love to own, or take the day off from work to get a massage, enjoy a lunch, then take a long walk in the park.

I am manifesting:

I am reflecting on:

THE WORLD THRIVES ON VARIETY.

I am grateful for:

Like driftwood floating downstream, negative thoughts may come. But just like the driftwood, they also float by. Allow them to float past you.

I am manifesting:

I am reflecting on:

**WHEN I FOCUS ON WHAT IS POSITIVE, I BRING
MYSELF CLOSER TO MY GREATEST SELF.**

DATE:

I am grateful for:

Your purpose in this universe is to grow and thrive in every way imaginable. Take a moment and imagine all the ways you can grow and thrive today.

I am manifesting:

I am reflecting on:

**MY EVOLUTION IS THE MOST NATURAL
THING IN THE UNIVERSE.**

I am grateful for:

The universe has planned so much greatness for you. Dream big about your possibilities, then remember that to dream about something is the first step in manifesting it.

I am manifesting:

I am reflecting on:

I DREAM MYSELF INTO BEING.

DATE: _____

I am grateful for: _____

_____

One. Step. At. A. Time.

I am manifesting: _____

_____

_____

I am reflecting on: _____

_____

_____

**I CAN OVERCOME ANY CHALLENGE
WITH THE RIGHT PERSPECTIVE.**

I am grateful for:

Rome wasn't built in a day, but it was imagined in an instant.

I am manifesting:

I am reflecting on:

**I AM REACHING FOR THE STARS WITH MY FEET
FIRMLY PLANTED ON THE GROUND.**

DATE:

I am grateful for:

Each person is born into the shared community of humanity, placed in the circle of being, and given a unique song. If a person transgresses, we must simply bring them back into the circle, and sing their song until they remember who they are.

I am manifesting:

I am reflecting on:

I CONTRIBUTE TO A COMMUNITY THAT HEALS.

DATE:

I am grateful for:

You are planting seeds today for the mighty oaks that will grow in the future. What is something that you can do today that will grow something big in your future?

I am manifesting:

I am reflecting on:

I TAKE SMALL STEPS TODAY TOWARD MY GREAT DESTINATION.

DATE:

I am grateful for:

Wellness is the byproduct of awareness. The more you practice cultivating awareness through observation and meditation, the more you will be directed toward wellness in body, mind, and spirit.

I am manifesting:

I am reflecting on:

THE UNIVERSE WANTS TO BLESS ME WITH ENERGY, VITALITY, AND A RICHNESS OF LIFE.

I am grateful for:

When people are in love, they are no longer two people but become one being, the composite of two hearts.

I am manifesting:

I am reflecting on:

**THE ONENESS OF THE UNIVERSE EXISTS
AS ONE BEATING HEART.**

DATE:

I am grateful for: _____

_____

You never stop growing. What are the ways that the universe is asking you to grow today?

I am manifesting: _____

_____

_____

I am reflecting on: _____

_____

_____

I AM NATURALLY EVOLVING INTO MY GREATEST BEING.

DATE:

I am grateful for:

Success and failure are the compass that will lead you to your destination. Can you perceive each success and failure as a pointer, leading you to your ultimate arrival?

I am manifesting:

I am reflecting on:

**EVEN FAILURES ARE LESSONS FROM THE UNIVERSE,
POINTING ME TOWARD MY ULTIMATE SUCCESS.**

DATE:

I am grateful for:

When you are in a room full of people, walking down the street, or standing in line, silently notice all the things you like about each person you see. Then, watch how the energy changes.

I am manifesting:

I am reflecting on:

GLOBAL CHANGE STARTS WITH ME.

DATE:

I am grateful for:

Be grateful for the challenges you have experienced in your life, because everything that has happened has brought you to this very moment.

I am manifesting:

I am reflecting on:

EACH GROWING PAIN REMINDS ME THAT
I'M GOING IN THE RIGHT DIRECTION.

DATE:

I am grateful for:

Nobody understands how incredible you are more than you do. What are the ways that you recognize your own brilliance?

I am manifesting:

I am reflecting on:

I AM A LIGHT BRIGHTENING THIS ENTIRE WORLD.

I am grateful for:

Close your eyes and quiet your mind. Take three long breaths. Listen to your body, mind, and spirit, then ask yourself what you need most in this moment in order to thrive.

I am manifesting:

I am reflecting on:

DEEP INSIDE, I KNOW WHAT IS BEST FOR MY OPTIMAL BEING.

DATE: _____

I am grateful for: _____

_____

Instead of judging something, try to be curious about it. Practice observing things from every facet.

I am manifesting: _____

_____

_____

I am reflecting on: _____

_____

_____

I HAVE THE POWER TO BE CURIOUS ABOUT ALL THINGS.

I am grateful for:

Your greatest gift to the world is the way you love the world. What do you love? Consider how, simply by loving those things, you bless the world.

I am manifesting:

I am reflecting on:

**TODAY, I CHOOSE TO SEE EVERYTHING
THROUGH THE FILTER OF THE HEART.**

DATE:

I am grateful for:

Do not try to be perfect. Simply do the next thing that will help you move in the right direction.

I am manifesting:

I am reflecting on:

**THERE ARE LIMITLESS GOOD THINGS
I CAN CHOOSE TO DO TODAY.**

DATE:

I am grateful for:

To get "there," you must learn to be "here"—and embrace the fact that "here" is always changing.

I am manifesting:

I am reflecting on:

EACH MOMENT ALONG THE JOURNEY IS AN OPPORTUNITY FOR A NEW ARRIVAL.

DATE:

I am grateful for:

Spend your time in the company of the people you most wish to emulate. You are the average of the five people with whom you spend the most time.

I am manifesting:

I am reflecting on:

**I CHOOSE TO ASSOCIATE WITH THOSE
WHO RAISE MY VIBRATION.**

DATE:

I am grateful for:

Nothing is impossible. Some things simply require greater imagination than others.

I am manifesting:

I am reflecting on:

DATE:

I am grateful for:

Practice eating your meals with complete presence, without being distracted by electronics or reading materials. Chew your food and savor each bite. After your meal, notice the way it made you feel.

I am manifesting:

I am reflecting on:

**MY HEALTHY CHOICES MAKE ME FEEL
VIBRANT, WELL, AND WHOLE.**

I am grateful for:

Close your eyes and take three long breaths. Speak to your heart and ask, "What is my purpose?" Listen for the response.

I am manifesting:

I am reflecting on:

I AM ON THE ROAD TO UNDERSTANDING MY DESTINY.

DATE:

I am grateful for:

Your heart contains more power than the biggest of challenges.

I am manifesting:

I am reflecting on:

MY HEART WILL SHINE THOUGH ANY DARKNESS.

DATE:

I am grateful for:

One must plan for joy in the journey toward any goal. Sometimes when you are unhappy at work, the problem is your relationship with the job as much as it is the work itself.

I am manifesting:

I am reflecting on:

THE JOURNEY IS THE DESTINATION.

DATE:

I am grateful for:

Sit upright, close your eyes, and take three deep breaths. Then breathe in and out rapidly, 10 times in a row. Pause for 10 seconds and do two more rounds of rapid breathing. Notice how this gives you energy for your projects.

I am manifesting:

I am reflecting on:

ALL THE ENERGY I NEED TO SUCCEED IS WITHIN ME.

I am grateful for:

Everything you consume—including food, water, sleep, music, news, social media, self-talk, and gossip—affects the frequency of your health vibration. Give yourself a full-spectrum health checkup today.

I am manifesting:

I am reflecting on:

**MY FUNDAMENTAL ESSENCE IS
THAT OF RADIANT WELLNESS.**

DATE:

I am grateful for:

Close your eyes and simply notice whatever lands in your field of awareness. Practice simply noticing and not judging.

I am manifesting:

I am reflecting on:

I DON'T NEED TO HAVE AN OPINION ABOUT EVERY THOUGHT AND FEELING.

I am grateful for:

The media we consume affects our energy, attitude, and optimism—and it can sometimes block our energy toward abundance. Try giving yourself a weeklong media fast:
no news, social media, magazines, or newspapers. Only read light fiction and listen to
uplifting music.

I am manifesting:

I am reflecting on:

MY SPIRIT CONSISTS OF WHAT IT CONSUMES.

I am grateful for:

Everything in the universe vibrates at its own frequency. Just like a radio dial, you can tune your frequency to receive and transmit that which reflects your highest good.

I am manifesting:

I am reflecting on:

I RADIATE MY FUNDAMENTAL WHOLENESS.

DATE:

I am grateful for:

Your relationships will be among the greatest teachers of your life. Be open to that wisdom and patient enough to learn their lessons.

I am manifesting:

I am reflecting on:

EVERY DAY, I AM OPEN TO THE KNOWLEDGE AND WISDOM OF LOVED ONES AND MENTORS.

I am grateful for:

The success you experience in your career is often dependent upon your success in your relationship with yourself.

I am manifesting:

I am reflecting on:

THE KEYS TO A SUCCESSFUL CAREER EXIST INSIDE OF ME.

I am grateful for:

Love is a lens that can bring anything into better focus. When confronted with an issue, sharpen your image by examining it through the lens of love.

I am manifesting:

I am reflecting on:

I AM LOVE.

DATE:

I am grateful for:

There has never been anyone like you. You possess gifts, insight, and experience unlike any other person.

I am manifesting:

I am reflecting on:

THE WORLD NEEDS ME TO SHARE MY GIFTS.

DATE:

I am grateful for:

Go out of your way to offer your gratitude to at least five people every day.

I am manifesting:

I am reflecting on:

MY GRATITUDE GENERATES GREATER ABUNDANCE.

DATE: _____

I am grateful for: _____

_____

Energy travels in the direction of thought. Focus on what you want, rather than what you don't want.

I am manifesting: _____

_____

_____

I am reflecting on: _____

_____

_____

I EXPECT MY BEST POSSIBLE LIFE TO UNFOLD.

DATE:

I am grateful for:

Talk to yourself the way you would talk to a trusted friend. After all, you are one.

I am manifesting:

I am reflecting on:

I SPEAK ONLY THE TRUTH.

DATE:

I am grateful for:

On a piece of paper, write your own biography as if you were the most important person who has ever lived. This allows you to envisage your true value and potential.

I am manifesting:

I am reflecting on:

I MAKE A DIFFERENCE ON THIS PLANET.

I am grateful for:

Like everything else in the universe, you are programmed to grow and evolve. How are you nurturing your own growth?

I am manifesting:

I am reflecting on:

**I'M GROWING INTO THE PERSON
I'M DESTINED TO BECOME.**

DATE: _____

I am grateful for: _____

_____

Make a list of the most exciting things that you'd love to learn before you die.

I am manifesting: _____

_____

_____

I am reflecting on: _____

_____

_____

**I EFFORTLESSLY VISUALIZE LIVING
MY LIFE EXACTLY AS I DREAM.**

DATE:

I am grateful for:

Success is not an absence of difficulty and failure. It is the act of continuing on regardless.

I am manifesting:

I am reflecting on:

I AM BECOMING STRONGER EACH DAY.

DATE:

I am grateful for:

Success cannot be measured by whether or not you have won, but rather by whether or not you can still sing at the end of the day.

I am manifesting:

I am reflecting on:

I HAVE ALREADY WON.

I am grateful for:

The universe has yet to reveal the most magnificent and miraculous parts of your being. Be open to what the universe has in store for you.

I am manifesting:

I am reflecting on:

MY ARMS ARE OPEN, READY TO RECEIVE WHAT THE UNIVERSE HAS PLANNED FOR ME.

DATE:

I am grateful for:

As you lie down at night, practice listing as many things as possible about yourself that you absolutely adore.

I am manifesting:

I am reflecting on:

I AM WORTHY OF LOVE.

I am grateful for:

False gatekeepers are those scary wooden statues that stand at the temple gates, deterring the faint of heart. But you are *not* the faint of heart.

I am manifesting:

I am reflecting on:

**I AM DETERMINED TO SUCCEED AND
ENJOY MYSELF ALONG THE WAY.**

DATE:

I am grateful for:

Your thoughts are powerful and will forecast your reality. Focusing on what you want sends energy in the right direction.

I am manifesting:

I am reflecting on:

MY THOUGHTS AND ATTITUDE GREATLY DETERMINE ANY OUTCOME.

DATE:

I am grateful for:

Your breath is the access point to universal energy. Notice your breath in this moment, and breathe life into everything you need to come alive today.

I am manifesting:

I am reflecting on:

I VIBRATE WITH THE HUM OF THE UNIVERSE.

DATE:

I am grateful for:

Remember that, of our baseline emotions, the one that is our birthright and origin is love. Everything else is a passing cloud.

I am manifesting:

I am reflecting on:

I ALLOW LOVE TO FILL MY LIFE IN EVERY POSSIBLE WAY.

I am grateful for:

Your perfect career is not gauged by how much money you make, but by how much satisfaction you derive from doing it, and whether it gives you the opportunity to share your gifts with the world.

I am manifesting:

I am reflecting on:

MY WORK IS MAKING A DIFFERENCE IN THE WORLD.

121

I am grateful for:

To attract the kind of love you wish to see, practice giving your love freely to every part of your life—including your work, friends, and neighbors.

I am manifesting:

I am reflecting on:

LOVE IS A BOOMERANG: AS I GIVE LOVE, IT ALWAYS COMES BACK.

DATE:

I am grateful for:

Write a love letter to yourself. On a piece of paper, list all of the things you adore about yourself, the difference you see yourself making in the world, and how grateful you are to be you.

I am manifesting:

I am reflecting on:

I LOVE MYSELF UNCONDITIONALLY.

DATE:

I am grateful for:

Your confidence and strength will be the two primary pathways that lead you to success.

I am manifesting:

I am reflecting on:

I HAVE WHAT IT TAKES TO SUCCEED.

I am grateful for: _____

_____

"Rock bottom" means that the only direction is up. Pretty soon, you'll realize that up is always the best option.

I am manifesting: _____

_____

_____

I am reflecting on: _____

_____

_____

**MY THOUGHTS ARE SHAPING ME INTO THE
PERSON I AM DESTINED TO BECOME.**

125

DATE:

I am grateful for: _____

_____

Your words are your truth, your bond, and your reality. How do you talk to yourself? And is it building you into the person you are destined to become?

I am manifesting: _____

_____

_____

I am reflecting on: _____

_____

_____

I USE MY WORDS TO BUILD MYSELF UP.

I am grateful for:

Practice acknowledging your personal victories every time you do something praiseworthy—whether it's winning the Nobel Prize or doing the dishes.

I am manifesting:

I am reflecting on:

I FREELY CELEBRATE MY SUCCESSES.

DATE:

I am grateful for:

What are the ways in which the world is asking you to grow physically, emotionally, or spiritually at this moment?

I am manifesting:

I am reflecting on:

I AM DESIGNED WITH A PROGRAM TO GROW AND LEARN.

DATE:

I am grateful for:

You are far more resilient than you imagine.

I am manifesting:

I am reflecting on:

I CAN DO THE NEXT RIGHT THING.

DATE:

I am grateful for:

Wake up to all the ways that you are winning in life, body, mind, and spirit. Expect success, and watch to see how you attract more of it.

I am manifesting:

I am reflecting on:

I AM THE SPIRIT OF SUCCESS.

I am grateful for:

Be an open cup, ready to receive the wisdom that the universe will undoubtedly pour into you.

I am manifesting:

I am reflecting on:

THE UNIVERSE IS OPENING ME IN UNIMAGINABLE WAYS.

DATE:

I am grateful for:

Sit, take a few deep breaths, and relax. Visualize the wise person you'll have become at the end of your life. Imagine what that version of yourself would tell you at this point in your life.

I am manifesting:

I am reflecting on:

**MY DEEPEST WISDOM IS ASKING ME
TO BE OPEN TO THE UNIVERSE.**

DATE:

I am grateful for:

Spend a few minutes each day taking an inventory of your body, mind, and spirit. Ask yourself if there is any way you could help yourself live a little bit better with ease.

I am manifesting:

I am reflecting on:

**SELF-CARE DOESN'T HAVE TO BE
DRAMATIC TO MAKE A DIFFERENCE.**

DATE:

I am grateful for:

Sit, close your eyes, and release any notion of good or bad, right or wrong. Take a few minutes and simply be the curious observer of a perceived challenge, obstacle, or problem in your life. After your brief meditation, rather than reacting to the situation at hand, ask yourself how you might respond.

I am manifesting:

I am reflecting on:

WHEN I RESPOND, RATHER THAN REACT, TO LIFE'S SITUATIONS, I OPERATE FROM MY HIGHEST INTELLIGENCE.

DATE:

I am grateful for:

Learn to focus and calm your energy by concentrating on your breath. Breathe deeply into your belly and feel your nervous system begin to relax. Once relaxed, envision all the things you wish for appearing in your life.

I am manifesting:

I am reflecting on:

I HOLD THE POWER TO BRING MY BEST LIFE INTO EXISTENCE.

DATE:

I am grateful for:

The gift of good work is the pleasure of sitting back and looking at something you've accomplished. Take a moment today to acknowledge the good work you're doing.

I am manifesting:

I am reflecting on:

GOOD WORK IS A GIFT TO MYSELF.

DATE:

I am grateful for:

The ability to love is a gift from the universe, even if the object or person you love is totally unaware.

I am manifesting:

I am reflecting on:

**THE ENTIRE UNIVERSE IS QUICKENED
WITH THE VIBRATION OF LOVE.**

DATE:

I am grateful for:

Make your entire life an expression of love. As you work on tasks throughout the day, practice repeating, "I am doing this out of love," and see how it changes your experience.

I am manifesting:

I am reflecting on:

LOVE MAKES THE UNIVERSE GROW.

DATE:

I am grateful for:

Before searching for the approval of others, seek your own approval. Then, boldly move forward in the direction that seems right.

I am manifesting:

I am reflecting on:

**I CHOOSE TO DIRECT MYSELF TO WHOLENESS, SO THAT
I MAY BE THE INSTRUMENT THE WORLD NEEDS ME TO BE.**

DATE:

I am grateful for: _____

_____

Make a list of your favorite personal gifts, accomplishments, and quirks. Then write, "My attributes make me unique, special, and incredible," next to each of them.

I am manifesting: _____

_____

_____

I am reflecting on: _____

_____

_____

THERE HAS NEVER BEEN ANYONE QUITE LIKE ME.

DATE:

I am grateful for:

Watch your thoughts, because they soon become your reality.

I am manifesting:

I am reflecting on:

DATE:

I am grateful for:

Speak to yourself the way a loving parent would guide a child—with encouragement, praise, and love.

I am manifesting:

I am reflecting on:

I'M TEACHING MYSELF TO WAKE UP TO MY HIGHEST SELF.

DATE:

I am grateful for:

If ever you feel like you are coasting in life, you're going downhill. Constantly grow into what you may become.

I am manifesting:

I am reflecting on:

**I AM GROWING INTO THE MIGHTY BEING
THAT I'M DESTINED TO BECOME.**

DATE:

I am grateful for:

Often, success simply means that it takes a larger and larger foe to beat you.

I am manifesting:

I am reflecting on:

DATE:

I am grateful for:

Sit and close your eyes. Take a few breaths. Meditate upon all the successes you've experienced in your life. Then apply that spirit to all the things you desire success for in the future.

I am manifesting:

I am reflecting on:

I HAVE THE POWER TO ATTRACT SUCCESS TO ME.

DATE:

I am grateful for:

The phrase "I don't know yet" is a magical door that invites the universe to teach you the next of its mysteries.

I am manifesting:

I am reflecting on:

I AM WILLING TO RECEIVE WHAT THE UNIVERSE HAS IN STORE FOR ME.

DATE:

I am grateful for:

Notice the way that you show up in your top five most important relationships. How are you making time, attention, and meaning in every relationship?

I am manifesting:

I am reflecting on:

**MY RELATIONSHIPS ARE AMONG
MY GREATEST RESOURCES.**

DATE:

I am grateful for:

Your work becomes immensely more satisfying when you can regularly employ your top five natural strengths. Reflect on what your greatest strengths are, and how you are using them in your work.

I am manifesting:

I am reflecting on:

I AM BLESSED WITH INCREDIBLE GIFTS.

DATE:

I am grateful for:

Take a macroscopic view of your work. How does the world benefit from what you do? Write down one statement about your purpose in the world regarding your work.

I am manifesting:

I am reflecting on:

DATE:

I am grateful for:

Sit and close your eyes. Take several deep breaths in and out through your nostrils. Visualize your breath moving into the areas of your life that you feel need vitality.

I am manifesting:

I am reflecting on:

I AM RIDING THE WAVE OF ENERGY IN MY LIFE.

DATE:

I am grateful for:

You must practice receiving love as much as you practice giving love.

I am manifesting:

I am reflecting on:

I am grateful for:

Confidence is not necessarily the product of always being right. Rather, it is the product of knowing that even when you're wrong, you'll still be okay.

I am manifesting:

I am reflecting on:

I WILL FIND MY WAY TO SUCCESS.

I am grateful for:

Sit, close your eyes, and take a few deep breaths. Spend several minutes visualizing all the wonderful things that you add to the world.

I am manifesting:

I am reflecting on:

THE WORLD IS LUCKY TO HAVE ME.

DATE:

I am grateful for:

When you encounter resistance, difficult feelings, or negative situations, practice visualizing all the ways that things can be different. Then, watch to see how things change.

I am manifesting:

I am reflecting on:

I AM CREATING MY OWN REALITY.

DATE:

I am grateful for:

Growing pains are inevitable. So is magnificence.

I am manifesting:

I am reflecting on:

155

DATE: _____

I am grateful for: _____

_____

Choose to practice something you're struggling with every day for five minutes. Each week, increase your practice time by five minutes. Watch yourself soon become an expert.

I am manifesting: _____

_____

_____

I am reflecting on: _____

_____

_____

PRACTICE DOES NOT NECESSARILY LEAD TO PERFECTION. BUT IT INEVITABLY LEADS TO PROGRESS.

DATE:

I am grateful for:

Sit, close your eyes, and take several deep breaths. Allow your breaths to resume their natural rhythm. Notice how easily the universe is pushing air into your lungs, without any effort on your part. You must simply allow yourself to be the life that the universe is pushing into you.

I am manifesting:

I am reflecting on:

THE UNIVERSE AND I ARE ONE.

DATE:

I am grateful for:

It's not *what* you wear, but *how* you wear it. Confidence is the most attractive part of your wardrobe.

I am manifesting:

I am reflecting on:

I'VE GOT THIS!

I am grateful for:

As you walk down the street or sit in a room full of strangers, practice thinking good thoughts about each person. Then, observe how many people are drawn to your open-hearted energy.

I am manifesting:

I am reflecting on:

**MY POSITIVE THOUGHTS ARE A REFLECTION
OF MY WHOLE BEING.**

DATE:

I am grateful for:

We all have good and bad seeds inside of us. You must simply choose to water the seeds you wish to grow.

I am manifesting:

I am reflecting on:

I AM GROWING EVERY DAY.

DATE:

I am grateful for:

Like bamboo, people are much stronger and more flexible than they initially appear.

I am manifesting:

I am reflecting on:

I AM EVEN MORE RESILIENT THAN I MAY KNOW.

161

I am grateful for:

Do something difficult today, knowing that you have the resiliency to grow from the experience.

I am manifesting:

I am reflecting on:

**MY STRUGGLES ARE HELPING ME GROW
INTO THE PERSON I MAY BECOME.**

I am grateful for:

Never give up. Success is right around the corner. Take it day by day and step by step. You'll discover that success was inside of you all along.

I am manifesting:

I am reflecting on:

I AM UNBEATABLE.

A Final Word

Congratulations! You've completed your *5-Minute Manifesting Journal*. It's no small feat to complete this journal. It is the product of determination, consistency, and a leveling-up of your own energy. Chalk this up as a personal victory!

Now that you've completed your journal, I invite you to read back through your entries and reflect on all the ways, big or small, that you may have grown. Revisit the moments of inspiration, optimism, and clarity you found. There were likely some entries that spoke to you more than others, and perhaps this was due to where you were in body, mind, and spirit on that particular day. I'm sure there were many moments of contemplation and illumination along the way. Hopefully, you have seen what a powerful impact a simple and consistent practice can have on your life.

Of course, completing this journal is just the beginning. I encourage you to practice manifesting every day and become an active participant in how your life unfolds. Some simple and effective practices to keep you on the pathway of manifesting include an ongoing gratitude practice, regular meditation (such as a daily five-minute session of focusing on your breath), and regular updates to your mood/vision board.

May you be happy, prosperous, and empowered to create the life you wish to make for yourself.

Resources

Other resources to help you learn more about manifesting.

***The Desire Factor* by Christy Whitman**
This book uses several actionable techniques, meditations, and tools to help you manifest and attract the things you want in your life.

***Life Visioning* by Michael Bernard Beckwith**
This book describes the four stages of getting out of a victim mindset and discovering your divine birthright as you manifest the life that you are meant to have.

River Writing
RiverWriting.com
A community-based writing and courage class that can help you develop a consistent and meaningful writing practice.

Scott Moore Yoga
ScottMooreYoga.com
Here you will find my blog, with articles that go into depth about many of the principles mentioned in this book, as well as downloadable recordings, courses, and meditations.

Acknowledgments

Immense love and gratitude to my wife, Seneca, who tirelessly supports me in every way, and who offered great insight, spirit, and encouragement throughout the writing of this book. Thank you to my son, Elio, for his sweet encouragement and love. Thank you to my many teachers, friends, students, and family members who have helped shape my soul, especially Taita Juanito, Peter Francyk, and Erin Geesaman Rabke. Special thanks to my dad and stepmom, Steve and RaNae, my twin brother Chris, and sister Lucy, as well as to Christy, John, Nan, Kim, Marit, Steve, Garrick, Meg, Jason, Liam, Lucy, Laurel, Greg, and Jim.

About the Author

 **Scott Moore** (E-RYT 500, RYS, YACEP, BA) is the author of *Practical Yoga Nidra* and has been teaching yoga and mindfulness since 2003. A former owner of multiple yoga studios, he loves teaching retreats, workshops, and teacher trainings, both in person and online. Scott was a professor at Westminster College and developed the curriculum for the accredited course "Yoga for Wellness," as well as for numerous treatment and reha-bilitation centers. Many people enjoy Scott's Yoga Nidra teachings and recordings on Insight Timer, Bandcamp, and YouTube. Scott writes for and has been featured in *Yoga Journal, Mantra Wellness, Origin Magazine, Yogi Times, Conscious Life News, Sivana East, Medium, Elephant Journal,* and his own blog at ScottMooreYoga.com. When he's not writing about, practicing, or teaching yoga or Yoga Nidra, he loves to play the saxophone, trail run, and spend time traveling with his family. He currently lives in Spain with his wife and son.